Mindset

Daily Laws

of

Money

Destiny S. Harris

. . .

Copyright

...

Dedication

To everyone who desires to improve their financial trajectory.

. . .

A Gift For You

Thank you for taking the time to read this book. As a token of my appreciation, here is a gift to you.

I give away free books daily. Here's how to get your free books today:

Step 1: Visit amazon.com/author/destinyharris

Step 2: Filter books by "Price: Low to High"

Step 3: Download available free eBooks

. . .

Table of Contents

. . .

Quick Bit

Thank you for taking the time to read this book.

My hope is that you leave at least 1% better than before you read this book and walk away with at least one takeaway.

I'd like to graciously ask that you help me by leaving a <u>review</u> of this book; your feedback helps me write better books and helps others capture a glimpse of the book.

With Kindness,
Destiny

. . .

Introduction

Money is a topic I'm deeply fond and passionate about -- thanks to my parents.

As kids, we read personal finance books as a family at the dinner table, used piggy banks religiously, set up our ROTH IRA accounts, and embarked upon many entrepreneurial ventures (with **strong** encouragement from our parents).

One thing I learned early on is that money is necessary, money creates opportunities, and money gives you more options.

I never desired to be broke or without money, which helped me master resourcefulness.

Though we read personal finance books at the dinner table, I never stopped learning about money.

I'm still learning about money today because I am a lifelong student.

There is much to learn and gain from the continuous acquisition of financial knowledge.

If more people educated themselves about money, they would experience more financial success.

In this book, you will read one theme split into miniature themes, all centered around money.

My hope is that this book will empower your financial outcomes exponentially and offer you foundational financial knowledge.

That's all I got.

...

Mindset

January 1

You Don't Need To Come From Wealth

"Wealth doesn't grow on trees. My family didn't come from wealth. I don't know anything about money. Earning money is hard. I don't know a thing about money. I'm not good at math. There is a ceiling on how much one can earn. I don't know how to earn more money."

Have you ever believed or believe any of these statements are true for you?

People frequently limit their financial outcomes based on their beliefs.

You don't need to come from wealth to experience or create wealth.

The only thing you need is the belief that you can create wealth and will create it.

How can one do this?

Education: the first step to attaining riches.

The most powerful wealth-creating tool is **applied** knowledge, which comes through educating yourself.

Book: Mindset - Think & Grow Rich For Black Women

. . .

January 2

Poverty Is A Gift

"Sometimes poverty is the greatest gift you can ever be given. Sometimes loss is the key that leads you to gain (Suze Orman)."

Something magical happens to those who choose to make something of themselves even though they're born with nothing or little nothing.

This group of people develops early an innate tenacity for personal and financial improvement; they will surrender this desire to improve for nothing

Those who choose to create wealth for themselves firmly believe that the universe has destined them to experience and have more.

Whatever you believe *becomes* your reality.

If you are born into poverty or fragile economic circumstances, this doesn't have to be your financial destiny.

The choice is yours whether or not you forge a new path of wealth, freedom, and options.

Article: Being Born In Fragile Economic Circumstances Is A Gift

...

January 3

Exposure Is Everything

My father gave me an invaluable gift: exposure to wealthy people, a wealthy lifestyle, and a wealthy mentality -- even though we didn't grow up wealthy.

I didn't come from wealthy circumstances, but my father had a side business with ultra-wealthy clients.

Tagging along with him on client jobs gave me the opportunity to communicate with his clientele in their homes; it also exposed me to homes I had never imagined possible in my lifetime.

I learned the value of exchanging your time for money at a relatively young age. There were times we would earn $200-$1000 per hour for our services.

Working on these jobs made it hard for me to maintain jobs in the fast food and retail industries that only offered $7.25/hour, but I'm thankful for these experiences; they taught me empathy, and more importantly, if I don't value my time, I will work jobs that prove this.

Exposing yourself to wealth, knowledge, and environments outside your comfort zone expands your mind and shows you another option.

Many people settle financially because they don't know a better way.

Get uncomfortable and expose yourself to wealthy individuals and environments. The more comfortable you become with wealth, the more of it you will attract into your reality.

Book: The Law of Attraction: Create Your Life

. . .

January 4

Educate Yourself At All Costs

I would not be where I am today without books.

My mother set timers for us as kids to read. We would frequently continue reading past the timer.

One of my favorite places to go was the library.

I'm still best friends with the library and get many of my books here.

My parents did a peculiar thing for me as a kid; we read personal finance books at the dinner table. The first book about money I remember reading was, "Rich Dad, Poor Dad," by Robert T. Kiyosaki.

We went on to read books by David Bach, Suze Orman, and Dave Ramsey, but my financial education didn't stop at the dinner table; it continued throughout my life. I'm still dedicated to learning and studying the game of money.

I can't imagine being the person I am today without books.

As a boss once told me, "Books are magical." Books will transform and evolve your being.

The more you learn, the more you earn.

Article: The Dinner Table Discussions About Money Impacted My Financial Trajectory For Life

. . .

January 5

Money Is Available to Everyone

Getting rich isn't reserved for a select few (Kathleen Elkins).

Money is an unlocked door that is always available and awaiting those who are ready and believe they can experience wealth.

Those who attract financial opportunities habitually create financial opportunities for themselves.

They don't sit and wait, hoping money will come to them one day. They don't invest all their hopes and dreams into a lottery ticket.

They create their own lottery ticket with consistent effort.

They solve problems for others and focus on continually providing value to others, which inevitably attracts more wealth, money, and financial independence into their lives.

Money isn't selective. It's a friend to anyone ready and willing to receive, lord over, and compound it.

Article: To Earn Above Average Dollars, You Must Shift & Expand Your Mindset

. . .

January 6

Eradicate Limiting Belief Systems

The average person has several old belief systems surrounding money that keep them in the same financial position.

Until people shift their thoughts and beliefs, they will continue to perpetuate the same financial results throughout their lives.

There is no way around these rules:

- If you have broke thoughts, you will remain broke.

- If you have broke habits, you will remain broke.

- If you manage your finances like a broke person, you will never escape the broke lifestyle.

People frequently say they desire a different financial outcome but are unwilling to shift their thoughts, habits, and actions.

What thoughts about money do you have that are self-defeating?

What financial habits do you have that are self-defeating?

Eradicate these thoughts and habits from your life immediately if you desire to transform your negative financial outcomes into positive ones.

Book: Mindset - Think & Grow Rich For Black Women

. . .

January 7

Wealth Is A Mindset

Wealth is a feeling that equates to always having more than enough and flourishing in every area of your life. There is no fear, doubt, or lack that infiltrates your thoughts.

Wealth is not just a money thing; it's a mentality.

How you think and what you think is attracting or detracting wealth from your life.

Think of someone you know who is always broke. How do you know they're broke?

Probably because they frequently complain about money, overdraft their accounts often, always seek discounts because they can't afford regular prices, live above their means, and never cease venting about their money problems.

We all know at least one person like this or has a few of these traits; they seem to always have a sad story (about money) and never seem to make much financial progress.

These people will never escape their reality until they shift their mindset, habits, actions, and thoughts.

Wealthy people think only in terms of abundance. There is no such thing as lack.

They recognize there is an unlimited supply of everything they need in the universe.

Furthermore, they know this rule applies to everyone, so they never compete against others or carry a scarcity mindset.

Article: Wealth Is Not Physical; It's A Mindset

January 8

If You Choose To Learn, Execute

"Knowledge is power only when put to use—
and then only when the use made of it is
constructive (David J. Schwartz)."

After reading one of the most influential
books, "The Magic of Thinking Big" by David
Schwartz, a friend complained that he didn't
have enough money to buy a cheap domestic
flight.

After reading a book like that, one of his first
questions should have been, **"How can I
afford to buy the plane ticket?"**

Books have magical powers, and infinite
knowledge can be found in the millions of
books available.

If you read a book, do yourself a favor and apply the knowledge.

Apply all the prudent knowledge you receive; if you don't, you stagnate, and it would be better if you hadn't read the book at all.

If you choose to learn, follow through on the responsibility to execute.

Article: Implement Knowledge To Eliminate Your Broke Mindset

. . .

January 9

Debilitating Mindsets

"Think you are weak, think you lack what it takes, think you will lose, think you are second class - think this way, and you are doomed to mediocrity (David J. Schwartz)

Four debilitating mindsets are the following:

1. Rich people obtain money illegally
2. I don't care about money
3. I hate money
4. There is not enough

People who don't like rich people, people who claim they don't care about money, people who hate money, and people who believe there is not enough money will always experience negative financial outcomes.

There is no way around it.

And if they happen to come into money, they will likely be poor stewards of it and lose it in some way.

Mindsets are powerful.

If you have a negative mindset, shift it before allowing it to continually produce unproductive results.

Article: 4 Mindset Types That Will Never Be Able To Build Wealth

. . .

January 10

Always Figure Out A Way To Afford It

Don't think, "I can't afford it." Instead, ask,
"How can I afford it

One of the most powerful questions you can ask yourself is, "How can I afford it?"

Many people give up their pursuit of something after they learn the price tag.

Determined financial outliers will always find a way to afford something because they are creative and do not allow themselves to be limited by a price tag.

Article: Lack Doesn't Exist; Only Abundance

. . .

January 11

Discover Your Wealth Mentality

There is more than enough. You have more than enough. Lack doesn't exist.

Something I learned very early in life is there are two types of people:

1. People with a scarcity mindset.
2. People with an abundance mindset.

People with scarcity mindsets struggle throughout their lives and never experience financial freedom.

They believe if one person or group of people are wealthy, they can't be wealthy.

People with abundance mindsets know if one person has wealth, they can experience wealth, too.

Money is a renewable source.

How much money you earn or come into contact with is solely limited by your beliefs.

Article: Discover Your Wealth Mentality

...

January 12

How You Handle Your Money Says A lot

The rich pay themselves first. The poor pay others first.

Observe the habits of those with money and those without money.

The average millionaire next door will never receive a paycheck and not pay themselves first.

People who have money will always prioritize investing and saving their money first and then paying everyone else last.

If you want to build wealth, you must practice the habit of paying yourself first.

People without money don't save or invest; they consistently spend their money on bills, essentials, or non-essentials before paying themselves.

If you never pay yourself, you will never have money.

Article: What Is The First Thing You Do With Your Money?

. . .

January 13

Be A Skillful Steward

"When prosperity comes, do not use all of it."
~Confucius~

Ever wonder where all your money went, and you still have two weeks left of the month?

We live in the age of "**buy it now; don't wait**" and **live in the moment.**

But these lifestyles only work if you can afford to do so.

If you're still learning how to afford to live this way while you're figuring it out, live below your means in the meantime.

Most people continue to live above their means because they don't understand how to be good stewards of their money.

Maybe they came from low economic status or never learned how to manage money.

The longer they continue to live above their means, the less likely they will build wealth.

It doesn't matter how much money you earn, but how much you keep.

Article: All You Have To Do Is Live Below Your Means To Be Financially Set

. . .

January 14

Increase Your Options Now

You're probably better off than you think.

If you ever want to gain perspective, watch a documentary on families or groups of people in places worse off than you yet still experience peace, happiness, and love.

After making a trip to India, I was reminded of how fortunate I am. Not to encourage comparing yourselves to others, but instead, be reminded of how little you need to survive.

Many add little conveniences here and there to make their lives "better" -- without considering the compounded costs of these items.

Moreover, we have so many "essentials" we subscribe to monthly without ever asking ourselves how much value they add to our lives.

Go through all of your bills and expenses today and cut out everything.

After 30 days of cutting off everything non-essential, determine what makes sense to add back.

You will likely find that you can experience satisfaction with less, which also puts money back into your pockets.

The more conscientious we are about the things we buy, the more financial freedom we give back to ourselves.

Instead of buying and consuming what everyone else is, ruthlessly question your desires.

Do you want it, or is society telling you to want it?

Cutting costs on things you "kind of want" creates more opportunities to save and invest -- leading to an accumulation of wealth.

The more frivolous our purchases, the more broke we tend to be.

People frequently make purchases without thinking, which is why most people will always be in debt, unable to afford a $500 emergency expense with cash, and not have enough for retirement when they reach that age.

Article: Cut Your Expenses For A Season To Give Yourself A Raise

...

January 15

Deviate From Your Past

*Most of the people I grew up around were
broke, and I never wanted to be like them.*

They say you become the average of the five
people closest to you; this might be true for
some, but I didn't always have physical access
to people above my level outside of books.

So, my most successful friends were often
authors of the books I read (without ever
meeting them).

I knew at an early age that I would always
have money. I started using a piggy bank at a
relatively young age; then, I saved up an
emergency fund and established a zero
balance in my checking account that I made

myself never spend. I was the loan shark people came to if they needed money.

There was never a time in my life when I needed to ask for a loan from family or friends.

If I needed additional funds, I found other ways to do it. If I had to take on debt, I quickly got out of it.

My past set me up to be either successful or unsuccessful.

Though we read personal finance books at the dinner table, I could have chosen not to follow the advice or take the subject matter seriously.

Instead, the subject resonated with me, and I continued investing in learning about it to create a different financial path for my future.

If you don't come from wealth, if your family is terrible with money, if you come from fragile economic circumstances, **deviate from it.**

It's a choice to have money.

It's also a choice not to have money.

Article: Trying To Be Like Average People Will Keep You Broke

...

January 16

Overspending Equates A Scarcity Mindset

People who spend more than they have are masterful <u>misusers</u> of their resources; they don't value money, leading to overspending, which is often a habit based on fear.

Why do people overspend?

Well, there are many reasons, but here are some of the common ones:

1. Their desires are out of control, and they never question these desires.

2. Delayed gratification is painful.

Most people don't want to wait for something when they can have it now (credit cards and loans made this possible).

3. People care more about what people think of them than they think of themselves.

People believe if they look the part, they will garner more respect, love, and admiration from others.

4. People who come into money frequently don't know how to manage it well, leading to poor spending habits.

Do you fall into any of these descriptions?

Article: Your Social Status Doesn't Trump Your Financial Freedom

. . .

January 17

Deviate From The Norm

Average people maintain average habits and produce average outcomes.

Most people produce average financial outcomes throughout their lives because they never invest in financial education, which would significantly improve their money.

I was chatting with my sister the other day and told her one of the best pieces of advice I've ever learned is to do the opposite of the masses.

Want to be successful with money?

Do the opposite of what most do with their money: deviate from the norm.

What do most people do with their money:

1. Spend more than they earn.

2. Upgrade their phones every 1-2 years.

3. Buy more house than they can afford, on top of getting a place with too much space.

4. Don't start investing when they're young.

5. Avoid **consistently** investing.

6. Don't read books about personal finance.

7. Leave their financial resources in the hands of others (e.g., family, financial advisors, spouses, etc.).

8. Don't budget or know how much money is coming in and out every month.

9. Don't enjoy talking about money and think it's an invasive subject.

10. Don't have a fully stocked emergency fund (3-12 months of expenses).

11. Can't cover a $500 emergency without a loan or credit card.

12. Pay the minimum payments on their debts.

13. Go to their graves with debt.

14. Don't have enough money saved up when they reach "retirement" age.

15. Are financially illiterate.

Want to be successful with money?

Do the opposite of the masses. That's all you have to do.

Article: 45 Things Most People Do With Their Money That You Should Avoid

. . .

January 18

Remove This Word From Your Vocabulary

Stop using the word "expensive;" it's a limiting word that defines your reality and financial outcomes.

As difficult as it might be to stop using the word "expensive," the word is severely limiting.

Whatever you define as expensive will usually remain just that for you -- out of reach.

A different phrasing to try: "It's a higher priced" or "That is overpriced."

Things are usually overpriced rather than priced high.

A perfect example: I stayed in a five-star resort with exceptional service versus another five-star resort with lesser service but a "stronger" brand.

The stronger brand would have been a good experience, but it's overpriced and not worth the investment.

The lesser-known brand offered a paradise-like experience for seven times less the price of the other five-star resort.

I have nothing to prove to anyone, so I don't need to invest in things I deem overpriced.

Article: Stop Saying Things Are Expensive

. . .

January 19

Brand Names Don't Equate Success

Why are the masses obsessed with name brands?

Far too many people in debt and barely have any money in their accounts are the same people with the nicest homes, nicest cars, nicest bags, nicest clothes, nicest shoes, and nicest life.

These people are willing to sacrifice their financial well-being for their appearances.

The masses believe name-brand things equate respect, status, adoration, and success, but real success doesn't require debt to fund it.

Furthermore, real success is never found in the things you own, but the person you are.

Rewire your brain to define success differently.

Success does not equal the things you can buy, the things you own, or the things you wear.

Success is the person you are, your options, and the **ability** to buy the things you want.

Article: Wealth Is Not Physical; It's A Mindset

...

January 20

Quit The Upgrade Lifestyle

Your iPhone works fine; what are you doing?

Here's my philosophy on phone upgrades:

If you can't purchase the upgrade with cash and have to sign up for an installment plan, you can't afford it, and you need to put the phone back and cancel your order.

People upgrade their iPhones because it feels good to have the latest and greatest, but upgrading your phone every year is a bit overdone.

If you can make the upgrade with cash, go for it, but be sure you're not upgrading because everyone else is doing it.

Question the practice.

Does this actually make sense?

Do I need to go through this process **every single** year?

Android people, I'm talking to you, too. You didn't think I forgot about you, did you?

Article: Stop Buying The New iPhone Every Year

. . .

January 21

There Is Enough

People have enough when they're grateful for what they have, spend less than they earn, and get creative.

Sometimes, the money is "tighter" than you'd like, but you don't have to go into scarcity mode and believe there isn't enough.

Instead, when money seems not to be present, focus on feeling grateful for the money you do have, spending less than you earn, and getting creative to create more resources for yourself.

There is **always** more than enough.

Money is a renewable resource; it never runs out.

More people are becoming millionaires than ever (even billionaires), proving there is enough.

Scarcity is only a predicament for those who believe in the concept.

Article: 10 Thoughts & Feelings That Will Prevent Financial Success

...

January 22

Do What Most People Don't Do

Barriers are meant to be obliterated.

I didn't follow the traditional route when it came to career and money.

Over time, I continue to increase my savviness through experimentation and questioning knowledge.

There are opportunities everywhere and in every field.

You may not see opportunity right off the bat.

Sometimes, opportunities come to you after you've been in a career for a while or around the right sources long enough to give you the right information.

Always pay attention to what everybody is doing, and what everybody is **not** doing.

Where can changes be made?

What is working and what isn't working?

What can you change in your own situation that would deviate from the norm but provide much success?

Article: Trying To Be Like Average People Will Keep You Broke

. . .

January 23

Average Minds Attract Average Rewards

You can't expect lucrative circumstances if your mind is broke.

There is a reason why there is a top 10%, and the majority falls into the other 90%.

Most people have average mindsets, which means most people have average money.

If you want to have higher-than-average finances, you need to have a higher-than-average mindset about money.

Do you believe your income is capped, or do you believe there isn't a limit?

Average minds believe in limits. Above-average minds obliterate limits.

How would you describe your mindset?

Article: Implement Knowledge To Eliminate Your Broke Mindset

...

January 24

Debt Is Normalized

It's normal to reach your grave carrying a load of debt.

It might be a car loan, a personal loan, a mortgage loan, a credit card loan, a business loan, a family loan, a student loan, or other loans, but everyone is likely to reach their grave in some kind of debt.

The normalization of debt has considerably continued to be on the rise.

Not only are people comfortable with debt, but they're comfortable adding to their debt loads and never paying it off.

It's no longer a big deal.

If everyone is doing it, why should you opt to be different?

Unless you use debt to create or increase wealth, debt is working against you.

The best motto when it comes to debt is to eradicate it sooner rather than later and avoid it when possible.

Do you want to owe someone money for the rest of your life?

You likely have family or friends who have borrowed money from you and never paid it back. How does that affect your relationship with them? How does that affect their credibility with you?

Article: Today, People Wait In Line To Go Into Debt

...

January 25

Financial Health Matters

Just because everyone sucks at money doesn't mean you fall into the same bucket.

For the most part, people will continually fail at money; they will stay in debt, live above their means, and remain primarily uneducated about how to manage their money effectively.

Why?

It's comfortable.

As long as a person gets by with a steady paycheck, they don't *need* to do any better.

But financial health matters just as much as your mental, physical, and emotional health.

What does financial health look like?

Living below your means.

Studying personal finance.

Keeping your expenses low.

Consistently increasing your income.

Consistently investing a percentage of your income.

Thinking long-term over short-term.

Article: What's Your Financial Health Status

. . .

January 26

Your Financial Mindset In Partnership

Relationships end because of everything, but especially money.

If you ask your average person what they're financially looking for in a partner, many will say they're seeking someone who can hold down a job and is bringing in a steady paycheck.

Others seek someone to financially provide everything so they don't have to worry about money or work.

In both of these cases, people set themselves up for financial failure.

Financial literacy and independence are the ultimate goals.

When you're seeking a partner, ensure you cover all the financial conversations that are most important to you.

Talk about debt, goals, income, how you want to share or keep finances separate, spending and savings habits (e.g., where do they spend their money, do they tend to save more than spend, how much they save, etc.), and everything else that matters to you.

Partner up with finances in mind. Don't wait until you're married or in a committed relationship to start talking about money.

Money is a crucial conversation. Have it sooner than later.

Article: Love And Money: Ask Your Partner The Questions Sooner
Than Later

. . .

January 27

Be Attracted To Financial Independence

Be different by being financially independent.

What is financial independence?

It's the ability to do what you want to do when you want to do it without having to work for anyone.

Some would argue financial independence is the length of time you can survive without bringing in additional income.

Most have zero financial independence because they live paycheck to paycheck.

How financially independent are you?

Article: Seek Financial Independence As If Your Life Depended On It

. . .

January 28

Study Everyone

Don't agree at first insight. Continue studying and questioning everything. Gather as much information as possible and then choose which beliefs and assumptions you will adopt.

Reading is the number one reason why I know about personal finance and how to manage my finances.

Without reading, I would know even less about investing, saving, budgeting, taxes, spending habits, and building wealth.

Most people never pick up a personal finance book because it's not "fun."

But how is not experiencing financial independence and having money not fun?

Study, pick apart, and learn from every financial guru available to you. Pick the stuff that applies best to you from everything you learn and act on it.

Article: 4% of Americans Read Personal Finance Books

. . .

January 29

When Will You Change?

If you never change, what will be your result?

Someone asked me to help pay their rent. I told them, "Not this time."

They had every reason **not** to be in the financial position they were in. They had multiple income sources.

They had low overhead.

They had the opportunity to stock away considerable money.

They didn't have the odds stacked against them.

After I told them "no," they developed a new habit of asking someone else until they started saying "no."

Patterns don't stop until you stop.

Article: Change Your Habits, Change Your Money

. . .

January 30

Release Hypnotic Rhythm

Breaking out of unproductive patterns requires a significant event.

Most people will never escape living paycheck to paycheck. Most people will never experience financial freedom.

It's not because they can't experience financial freedom; it's because they are addicted to their patterns.

Patterns are difficult to escape, difficult to release, and difficult to replace.

What will it take to break out of your financial patterns that aren't producing optimal results?

For me, it was seeing family, friends, and strangers constantly struggle and complain about money. I never wanted that to be my experience, so I invested considerable time and effort into financial education.

But most importantly, I developed the early habit of living below my means and avoiding an addiction to materialism.

Article: 12 Unhealthy Money Habits You Should Quit Now

. . .

January 31

Two Types

Those who have. Those who don't have.

There will always be two types of people:

The ones who have.
The ones who don't have.

The ones who have, have developed a mechanism within their minds that attracts money into their lives; they're also willing to put in effort to bring money into their lives.

If you're unsatisfied with your financial results, what are you willing to do to change the narrative?

What are you willing to stop believing to cultivate the proper frame of mind?

Article: To Become Wealthy, You Must Start Thinking Wealthy NOW.

Thank You For Reading

Thank you for reading this book.

Stay loved, blessed, lucky, favored, aware, joyous, and committed to bettering yourself.

...

The End.

...

About Destiny S. Harris

Destiny S. Harris' goal is to positively inspire, cultivate, elevate, and educate the minds of individuals across the globe through her writing.

Creating (whether books, courses, articles, poetry, or music) has always been Destiny's thing, not to mention health & fitness and all things entrepreneurial.

Destiny published her first book, "Beauty Secrets for Girls," at age 11 and her second book, "Don't Wait Until It's Too Late," at age 12.

Destiny obtained three degrees in Psychology, Political Science, & Women's Studies. She also started her own music teaching business at the age of 14, which she led for over ten years. In addition, she has been teaching academic, career, and personal development topics to thousands of students and readers since 2004.

Outside of writing, Destiny loves and enjoys a few other things: reading, weightlifting, walking, biking, traveling, football, dogs, animals, food, classic movies, mountain and ocean views, sleeping, plants, and nature.

Check out her work, leave a review, share your thoughts with your friends and family, and be a part of a movement: helping people learn and grow through means of self-education (books).

Complete the Steps To Get Free eBooks:

Step 1: Go to amazon.com/author/destinyharris

Step 2: Filter books by "Price: Low to High"

Step 3: Download available free books

. . .

Connect W/ Destiny S. Harris

Please reach out and stay in touch. Start a conversation today @ destinyh.com

. . .

Free Gifts!

Access courses & free eBooks at the link below:

destinyh.com

...

Please Leave A Review

If this book impacts you in some way, please let me know by dropping a review on it.

I write better books with **your** input.

. . .

Tell Me What You Want

*I've written many books, but if you don't see
what you're looking for or need, get in touch
with me via my website, articles, comments, or
reviews, and let me know what you're looking
for so I can create it for you.*

I'm here to serve,

Destiny

. . .